C IS FOR CHINA

by Robyn Chance
Illustrated by Robyn Chance

Text copyright © 2012 Robyn Chance
Illustration copyright © Robyn Chance
The beautiful photo for the B is for Buddha illustration was based on a photograph used with permission by Don Farber.

All rights reserved. No part of this publication may be preproduced or transmitted in any form or by any means, electronic, photo-copying, recording, or otherwise, without the prior written permission of the publisher.

The illustrations are rendered in watercolor.

10 9 8 7 6 5 4 3 2 1 0

ISBN-13 Paperback: 978-1-48488493-35-0
      Kindle: 978-1-63003-590-7
      EPDF: 978-1-936850-33-4

Emmalee Xin

According to ancient Chinese belief, you were born with an invisible red thread that connected you to all the people who would play a part in your life; people who you were fated to be with. I am so grateful that a red thread exists between us. With all my love, this book is dedicated to you.

In July 2006, my family embarked upon an amazing journey that led us to our beautiful daughter, Emmalee. She was living in an orphanage in Sichuan, China, in a small village known as Yibin. The journey was full of all kinds of challenges, but most journeys that carry meaning and importance in our lives are.

When I returned to the States, I was filled with inspiration. I wanted to write a children's book that really touched on some of China's history, mythology, language and character. I wanted it to be for Emmalee, as well as for all children of the world. After I wrote *C is for China*, I began illustrations for each page. The cover is inspired by a picture I took of Emmalee at the White Swan Hotel in Guangzhou, and is enhanced with many of the culturally relevant images that make up parts of China.

I am excited to share what I have learned of China's rich culture, with other families. I hope you enjoy C is for China.

As you read the book, look for Chinese characters that appear on each illustration. The Chinese character that appears on each page represents the main idea presented in that narrative. For example, the symbol here: is for Asia—the red stamp on the illustration is my Chinese chop, the traditional stone seal used for names. It is how I have signed my artwork in this book.

C IS FOR CHINA

A IS FOR ASIA, a place large and wide.
It holds many things in its vast countryside.
It's a land old and new that continues to grow,
With rivers and valleys and mountains with snow.

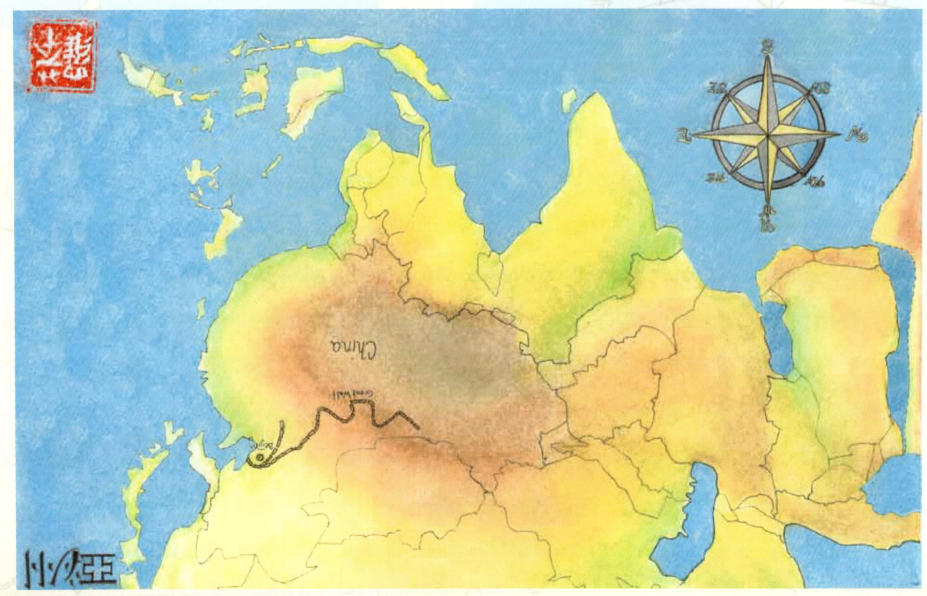

B IS FOR BUDDHA, who's found in many places.
He treasured all people, regardless of races.
His message to all is to stay in the present.
To be still and to listen can be very pleasant.

C IS FOR CHINA, a country quite grand.

It's full of rich history, a beautiful land.
The people so friendly, the cities so bright.
The mountains are glorious. You should see it at night.

D IS FOR DRAGON, a mythical beast.
Snake-like, with claws, it is found in the East.
Powerful and strong, like the emperors of old.
Its job was to protect, China's traditions to uphold.

E IS FOR EMPERORS, who ruled China long ago.
They were part of great dynasties that helped the country grow.
Dragons represented them, to show their strength and skill.
Now, their leadership has changed because time does not stand still.

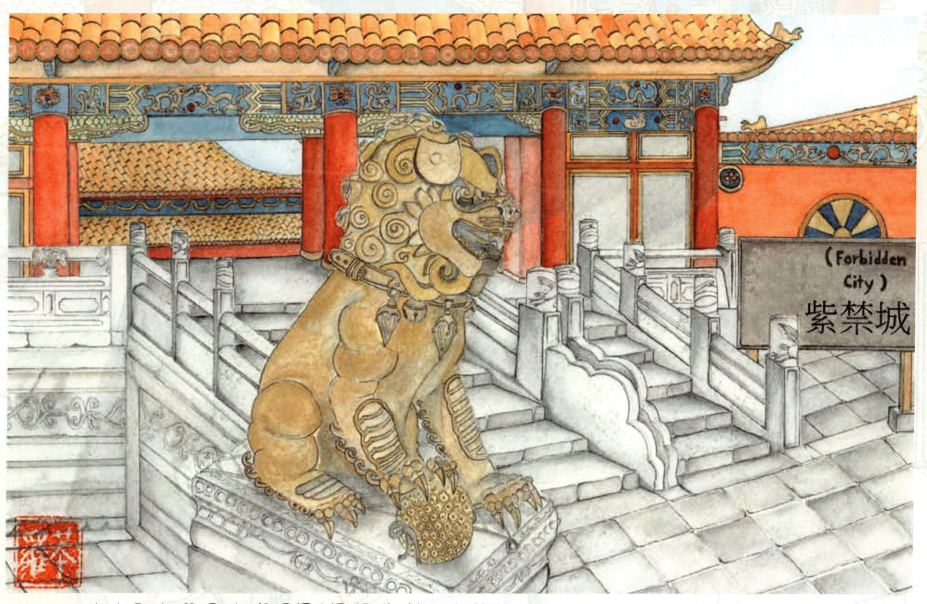

F IS FOR FORBIDDEN CITY, it's where the Emperor lived.
People would go there to seek the guidance that he would give.
It's surrounded by walls and strange mythical things,
Like dragons and lions and creatures with wings.

G IS FOR THE GREAT WALL, which took years to create.
It was built for protection, and is anything but straight!
It careens through the mountains and dives through the valleys.

It was made from strong stone and it has many alleys.
Steep, narrow and long, it has been there for years.
People now visit it and buy souvenirs.

H IS FOR HAO (HOW), a mystical creature.

Though it represents union, it has more than one feature.
Its body is a phoenix and its head is a dragon.
It's on a perch by the door, but it's not a welcome wagon.
It's there for protection and to be a guide.
The Emperor would consult it before he went outside.

I IS FOR INVENTIONS, and interesting facts.
China's rich history is full of great acts!
They invented the wheelbarrow, kites and printing;
But that isn't all—it's only the beginning.
They created the compass and calligraphy, too.
It's amazing how much the Chinese people knew!

J IS FOR JADE, a special kind of stone.
It comes in different colors, but for green it's best known.
It's carved into jewelry, statues and dishes.
Some believe its power can help answer people's wishes.

K IS FOR KUNG FU, one of the martial arts.
The skill was developed by studying animal parts,
Like the pounce of the tiger, or the stance of a crane.
To perform it correctly, one really must train.

語言

L IS FOR LANGUAGE. In China there are many.
Though most speak Mandarin, there are dialects aplenty.
There are one billion people who speak some form of Chinese.
It's the number one language spoken throughout the seven seas.

M IS FOR MARKETS, where people sell things;
From herbs to silk dresses to beautiful rings.
Theses shops are in alleys and sometimes in squares,
So merchants in China can barter their wares.

N IS FOR NEW MOON, which starts China's New Year,
A grand celebration the people hold dear.
It begins in their spring and lasts fifteen days.
There are fireworks, dances and delicious buffets.

O IS FOR OLYMPIC GAMES, where top athletes do compete.
They come from around the world, and this is where they meet.
Different countries get to host them, and China had its turn.
So the world could watch them contend for the medals they might earn.

熊貓

P IS FOR PANDA, a national treasure.
They eat bamboo and sit around for pleasure.
Most have black-and-white fur, though some are red.
The world really loves them and in China they are bred.

18

Q IS FOR QIN DYNASTY, which lasted fifteen years.
When the Emperor was buried, he was guarded, it appears.
An army of clay soldiers to protect him were made.
They've lasted thousands of years and that is where they've stayed.

R IS FOR RICE, a yummy, tiny grain
That grows in water and likes lots of rain.
There are many different kinds that people like to eat.
It goes so well with many meals. It really is a treat.

S IS FOR SYMBOLS—They're important, as you'll see.
The Chinese use them in their writing and in their art quite frequently.
Animals in particular play important parts.
Their characters help us know each other and the dreams within our hearts.

T IS FOR TAOISM, a balanced way of living.
It was created by Lao Tzu, a man who was giving.
It strives to find harmony and stay "in the flow."
Once you find it, it's said that you will know.

U IS FOR UNIQUE, which describes Chinese history.
It is long and varied, with parts still a mystery.
There have been many leaders and industry has changed.
Though the people's lives are different, some traditions have remained.

Confucius 孔子　價值　Buddha 菩薩

Lao-Tzu 老子

V IS FOR VALUES—in China these are strong.
To be there for your family and always right a wrong.
Confucius, Tao and Buddha help people on their quest
To earn the respect of others and always do their best.

W IS FOR WRITING, which in China is unique.
They use symbols called characters that require a special technique.
Strokes are used to create them; twelve main ones are the keys.
The combinations are endless, but you must know them to read Chinese.

新

XIN, PRONOUNCED "SHIN," means "new" in Chinese.
Though, it means something more to me, if you please.
It is the name of my daughter, who came from Sichuan.
She is a beautiful child whom I love to kiss on.

Y IS FOR YIN YANG, which means forces that push and pull.
They seem to work against each other, but they really make a whole.
One needs the other, just like the night needs the day.
The world is mysterious, but it's balanced in its way.

再見

Z IS FOR ZAIJIAN, which in Chinese means "bye-bye."
It's the traditional way of leaving, just like Ni-hao means "hi."
Learning some Chinese is a good thing to do.
There are many Chinese people who would like to say "hi" to you.

Xuéhui shuō Zhōng wén 学会讲中文

Pronounced: Shay hooway show Chong when

(Learn to speak Chinese)

你好	Nǐ hǎo	(KNEE how)	Hello and How are you?
再见	Zàijiàn	(sigh jyen)	Goodbye
四川	Sichuān	(Su chuan)	A Province Of China
我爱你	Wǒ ài nǐ	(woo i knee)	I love you
我很开心	Wǒ hěn gāoxing	(Woo hun kigh shin)	I am happy
非常好	fēicháng hǎo	(fay chung how)	Very good
母亲	mǔqīn	(MOO chin)	Mother
父亲	fùqīn	(FU chin)	Father
家庭	jiātíng	(jya ting)	Family
好的	hǎo de	(how duh)	yes
不	bù	(boo)	no
请	qǐng	(ching)	please
谢谢	xièxie	(shyeah shyeah)	thank you
不必客气	bùkèqi	(boo kuh-chee)	you are welcome
晚安	wǎn´ān	(wan un)	good night

ACKNOWLEDGMENTS

Thank you to EVERYONE who helped make this book happen! I would especially like to thank my husband David and my beautiful children, my mom Anita Solt, Megan Chance, Lisa Coyne, Kara Klotz and all of the wonderful people and organizations that work to make forever families happen!

ABOUT THE AUTHOR

Robyn Chance lives in Olympia, Washington, with her family, including two cats and a dog. She is a teacher and an artist. Over the years she has developed a real passion for telling stories about the enchanting world in which we live. Her goal is to help children explore and become curious about the world around them. In addition to writing and illustrating books and working on a variety of artistic endeavors, Robyn loves to travel and learn new things. She loves to be outdoors and is really seriously thinking about moving to a sunnier place, maybe Spain or Italy, she isn't sure yet.